Nurse

Career Assessments and Their Meanings

Childcare Worker

Clergy

Computer Programmer

Financial Advisor

Firefighter

Homeland Security Officer

Journalist

Manager

Military and Elite Forces Officer

Nurse

Politician

Professional Athlete and Sports Official

Psychologist

Research Scientist

Social Worker

Special Education Teacher

Veterinarian

Careers with Character

Nurse

by Rae Simons and Viola Ruelke Gommer

MASON CREST PUBLISHERS

Mason Crest Publishers Inc.
370 Reed Road, Broomall, Pennsylvania 19008
(866) MCP-BOOK (toll free)
www.masoncrest.com

First Edition, 2003
13 12 11 10 09 08 07 06 05   10 9 8 7 6 5 4 3

Library of Congress Cataloging-in-Publication Data

Simons, Rae.
  Nurse / by Rae Simons and Viola Ruelke Gommer.
     v. cm. — (Careers with character)
Includes bibliographical references and index.
Contents: Introduction — Job requirements — Integrity and trustworthiness — Respect and compassion — Justice and fairness — Responsibility — Courage — Self-discipline and diligence — Citizenship — Career opportunities.
  ISBN 1-59084-319-3
        1-59084-327-4 (series)
  1. Nursing—Vocational guidance—Juvenile literature. [1. Nursing—Vocational guidance. 2. Vocational guidance.] I. Gommer, Viola Ruelke. II. Title. III. Series.
  RT82.S62 2003
  610.73'023—dc21
                              2002154668

Produced by Harding House Publishing Service, Vestal, N.Y.
www.hardinghousepages.com
Design by Lori Holland.
Composition by Bytheway Publishing Services, Binghamton, New York.
Printed in the Hashemite Kingdom of Jordan.

Photo Credits:
Corbis: pp. 54, 55, 56, 57, 58, 60, 61, 62, 63, 66, 68, 69, 70, 71, 74, 76, 77, 79, 80, cover
Corel: pp. 29, 39, 40
PhotoDisc: pp. 4, 9, 11, 16, 18, 20, 21, 22, 23, 28, 31, 36, 38, 41, 47, 48, 49, 52

CONTENTS

We each leave a fingerprint on the world.
Our careers are the work we do in life.
Our characters are shaped by the choices
we make to do good.
When we combine careers with character,
we touch the world with power.

INTRODUCTION

by Dr. Cheryl Gholar
and Dr. Ernestine G. Riggs

In today's world, the awesome task of choosing or staying in a career has become more involved than one would ever have imagined in past decades. Whether the job market is robust or the demand for workers is sluggish, the need for top-performing employees with good character remains a priority on most employers' lists of "must have" or "must keep." When critical decisions are being made regarding a company or organization's growth or future, job performance and work ethic are often the determining factors as to who will remain employed and who will not.

How does one achieve success in one's career and in life? Victor Frankl, the Austrian psychologist, summarized the concept of success in the preface to his book *Man's Search for Meaning* as: "The unintended side-effect of one's personal dedication to a course greater than oneself." Achieving value by responding to life and careers from higher levels of knowing and being is a specific goal of teaching and learning in "Careers with Character." What constitutes success for us as individuals can be found deep within our belief system. Seeking, preparing, and attaining an excellent career that aligns with our personality is an outstanding goal. However, an excellent career augmented by exemplary character is a visible expression of the human need to bring meaning, purpose, and value to our work.

Career education informs us of employment opportunities, occupational outlooks, earnings, and preparation needed to perform certain tasks. Character education provides insight into how a person of good character might choose to respond, initiate an action, or perform specific tasks in the presence of an ethical dilemma. "Careers with Character" combines the two and teaches students that careers are more than just jobs. Career development is incomplete without character development. What better way to explore careers and character than to make them a single package to be opened, examined, and reflected upon as a means of understanding the greater whole of who we are and what work can mean when one chooses to become an employee of character?

Character can be defined simply as "who you are even when no one else is around." Your character is revealed by your choices and actions. These bear your personal signature, validating the story of who you are. They are the fingerprints you leave behind on the people you meet and know; they are the ideas you bring into reality. Your choices tell the world what you truly believe.

Character, when viewed as a standard of excellence, reminds us to ask ourselves when choosing a career: "Why this particular career, for what purpose, and to what end?" The authors of "Careers with Character" knowledgeably and passionately, through their various vignettes, enable one to experience an inner journey that is both intellectual and moral. Students will find themselves, when confronting decisions in real life, more prepared, having had experiential learning opportunities through this series. The books, however, do not separate or negate the individual good from the academic skills or intellect needed to perform the required tasks that lead to productive career development and personal fulfillment.

Each book is replete with exemplary role models, practical strategies, instructional tools, and applications. In each volume, individuals of character work toward ethical leadership, learning how to respond appropriately to issues of not only right versus wrong, but issues of right versus right, understanding the possible benefits and consequences of their decisions. A wealth of examples is provided.

What is it about a career that moves our hearts and minds toward fulfilling a dream? It is our character. The truest approach to finding out who we are and what illuminates our lives is to look within. At the very heart of career development is good character. At the heart of good character is an individual who knows and loves the good, and seeks to share the good with others. By exploring careers and character together, we create internal and external environments that support and enhance each other, challenging students to lead conscious lives of personal quality and true richness every day.

Is there a difference between doing the right thing, and doing things right? Career questions ask, "What do you know about a specific career?" Character questions ask, "Now that you know about a specific career, what will you choose to do with what you know?" "How will you perform certain tasks and services for others, even when no one else is around?" "Will all individuals be given your best regardless of their socioeconomic background, physical condition, ethnicity, or religious beliefs?" Character questions often challenge the authenticity of what we say we believe and value in the workplace and in our personal lives.

Character and career questions together challenge us to pay attention to our lives and not fall asleep on the job. Career knowledge, self-knowledge, and ethical wisdom help us answer deeper questions about the meaning of work; they give us permission to transform our lives. Personal integrity is the price of admission.

The insight of one "ordinary" individual can make a difference in the world—if that one individual believes that character is an amazing gift to uncap knowledge and talents to empower the human community. Our world needs everyday heroes in the workplace—and "Careers with Character" challenges students to become those heroes.

Nursing is a career that requires expertise based on education, experience—and character.

1

JOB REQUIREMENTS

*Success requires education,
experience—and character.*

With a tired sigh, Latasha finished changing an elderly woman's bandages. The woman was only one of the many patients who had made their way to the emergency room of the Manor Lake Hospital. The hospital was located in a small town outside Chicago, and it was usually busy on Friday and Saturday nights. Tonight was no exception.

Thinking she could take a break for a few minutes, Latasha went to the staff lounge to get off her feet. As she settled down onto one of the chairs, she heard the blare of the intercom: *"All nurses report to the ER, stat! A multivehicle accident with at least a dozen victims is on its way. ETA is two minutes!"*

Latasha didn't think twice about how tired she was; she jumped up and ran down the hall to the emergency room to wait for the ambulances that would be rolling in any moment. Her tired and aching body felt suddenly alive. She knew patients would be needing her, and she felt a sense of duty to give them her best.

As an emergency room nurse, Latasha is just one of the many nurses who were busy that night in all the wards of Manor Lake Hospital. Nurses are the foundation of the daily functioning of any hospital; from the operating rooms to the **obstetric** floor, and from **pediatrics** to the **psychiatric** wing, the hospital could not operate without nurses. Across the United States and Canada, nurses play an essential role in the entire medical system.

There are two major types of nurses: registered nurses (known as RNs) and licensed practical nurses (LPNs). LPNs are sometimes referred to as registered practical nurses (RPNs) in some provinces of Canada.

Registered Nurses

Registered nurses work to promote health, prevent disease, and help patients cope with illness. They are advocates and health educators for patients, families, and communities. When providing direct patient care, they observe, assess, and record symptoms, reactions, and progress; assist physicians during treatments and examinations; administer medica-

The History of Nursing

The profession of nursing has existed for centuries, although not in the form we know today. Wealthy women who lived in the early days of Christianity created hospitals to care for the ill; they were known as deaconesses. For centuries afterward, however, men were nurses, and at the end of the Crusades a male nursing order known as the Knights Hospitallers was created. Still more centuries later, Vincent DePaul, a parish priest, organized the Sisters of Charity, who today continue to run some of the finest hospitals in the world; Vincent DePaul laid the foundation for modern nursing. Fast-forward again through history, and you will find a young woman by the name of Florence Nightingale, who vowed to improve the hospital conditions and patient care. She paved the way for women to become professionals in this profession of caring.

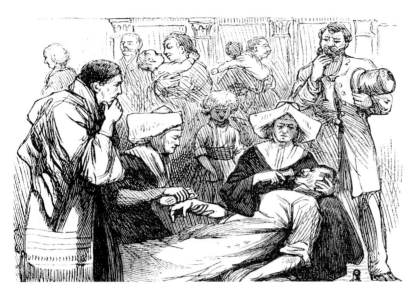

Long ago, nursing was done almost entirely by the church.

tions; and provide support in **convalescence** and rehabilitation. RNs also develop and manage nursing care plans; instruct patients and their families in proper care; and help individuals and groups take steps to improve or maintain their health. While state laws govern the tasks that RNs may perform, the work setting usually determines nurses' daily job duties.

Hospital nurses form the largest group of nurses. Most are staff nurses, who provide bedside nursing care and carry out medical **regimens**. They may also supervise licensed practical nurses and nursing aides. Hospital nurses are usually assigned to one area, such as surgery, maternity, pediatrics, emergency room, intensive care, or treatment of cancer patients. Some may rotate among departments.

Office nurses care for outpatients in physicians' offices, clinics, **surgicenters**, and emergency medical centers. They assist with examinations, administer injections and medications, dress wounds and incisions, help with minor surgery, and maintain records. Some also perform routine laboratory and office work.

Registered Nurse (RN)

RNs go to college for two to four years. They are usually team leaders on a ward. RNs look after the general care of patients:

- administering drugs.
- monitoring and analyzing vital statistics.
- receiving and carrying out physicians' orders.
- educating patients on an in-depth level.

Licensed Practical Nurse (LPN)

LPNs typically work under the supervision of an RN. Their license requires only about one year of schooling. Some people choose to become LPNs with the intention of completing their RN course work later. Normally, LPNs look after the general care of a patient:

- administering some type of drugs.
- carrying out physicians' orders under the direction of an RN.
- monitoring vital statistics.
- educating patients on a basic level.

Nursing home nurses manage nursing care for residents with conditions ranging from a bone fracture to ***Alzheimer's disease***. Although they often spend much of their time on administrative and supervisory tasks, RNs also assess residents' health conditions, develop treatment plans, supervise licensed practical nurses and nursing aides, and perform difficult procedures such as starting intravenous fluids. They also work in specialty-care departments, such as long-term rehabilitation units for patients with strokes and head injuries.

Home health nurses provide services to patients at home. After assessing patients' home environments, they care for and instruct patients and their families. Home health nurses work with a broad range of patients, such as those recovering from illnesses and accidents, cancer, and childbirth. They must be able to work independently, without any direct supervision; they also may need managerial skills for supervising home health aides.

Public health nurses focus on populations, working with individuals, groups, and families to improve the overall health of communities. They also work as partners with communities to plan and implement programs. Public health nurses instruct individuals, families, and other groups regarding health issues, disease prevention, nutrition, and childcare. They arrange for immunizations, blood pressure testing, and other health screening. These nurses also work with community leaders, teachers, parents, and physicians in community health education.

Occupational health or *industrial nurses* provide nursing care at worksites to employees, customers, and others with minor injuries and illnesses. They provide emergency care, prepare accident reports, and arrange for further care if necessary. They also offer health counseling,

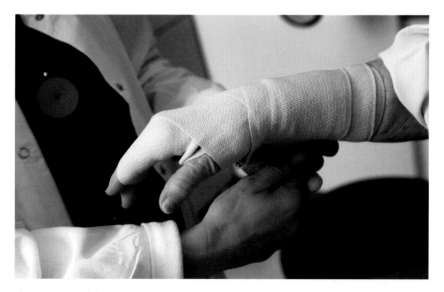

Occupational health nurses may provide worksite care for minor injuries such as sprained wrists.

Most registered nurses work in well-lighted, comfortable healthcare facilities. Home health and public health nurses travel to patients' homes, schools, community centers, and other sites. Nurses may spend considerable time walking and standing. Patients in hospitals and nursing homes require 24-hour care; consequently, nurses in these institutions may work nights, weekends, and holidays. RNs also may be on-call (available to work on short notice). Office, occupational health, and public health nurses are more likely to work regular business hours.

assist with health examinations and inoculations, and assess work environments to identify potential health or safety problems.

Head nurses or *nurse supervisors* direct nursing activities. They plan work schedules and assign duties to nurses and aides, arrange for training, and visit patients to observe other nurses and ensure the proper delivery of care. They may also see that records are maintained and that equipment and supplies are ordered.

What It Takes to Become a Successful Nurse

According to a survey in the *American Journal of Nursing*, nurses need the following qualities to succeed:

• the ability to work under pressure.
• good physical stamina.
• people skills.
• manual dexterity.
• leadership ability.
• problem solving skills.

For registered nurses in all states, as well as Canada, students must graduate from an approved nursing program and pass a national licensing examination to obtain a nursing license. Nurses may be licensed in more than one state, either by examination, by endorsement of a license issued by another state, or through a multistate licensing agreement. All states require periodic license renewal, which may involve continuing education. The Canadian Nurses Association also offers a certification credential, based on

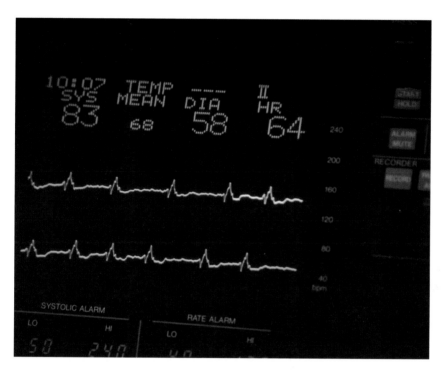

Today's technology has contributed in countless ways to the field of nursing.

Nurses with the U.S. Public Health Service Commissioned Corps Readiness Force respond to the country's emergency medical needs. In 2001, this meant they reassured anthrax-exposed postal workers and tended weary firefighters after the terrorist attacks of September 11. Every year, the corps responds to at least nine events; some, like a presidential inauguration or the Olympics, are planned ahead of time, but most, like hurricanes, floods, and wildfires, are not. The corps is there for the big events that make the news—and for smaller emergencies as well (like when the staff at a small, 22-bed, Alaskan Indian Health hospital all caught the flu).

passing a national exam, which is designed to promote excellence in nursing.

Three major educational paths can lead to registered nursing: an associate degree in nursing (A.D.N.), a bachelor of science degree in nursing (B.S.N.), or a diploma. The A.D.N. programs, offered by community and junior colleges, take about two to three years. About half of the 1,700 RN programs in the year 2000 were at the A.D.N. level. The B.S.N. programs, offered by colleges and universities, take four or five years. More than one-third of all programs in 2000 offered degrees at the bachelor's level. Diploma programs, offered by hospitals, take two to three years to complete. Only a small number of programs offer diploma-level degrees. Generally, licensed graduates of any of the three program types qualify for entry-level positions as staff nurses.

Licensed Practical Nurses

Licensed practical nurses care for the sick, injured, convalescent, and disabled under the direction of physicians and registered nurses. Most LPNs provide basic bedside care. They take vital signs such as temperature, blood pressure, pulse, and respiration. They also treat bedsores,

According to character education expert Tom Lickona, good character depends on possessing certain core values— qualities like respect and compassion, self-discipline and diligence, responsibility, and courage. Other aspects of good character include integrity and trustworthiness, justice and fairness, and citizenship. These values affirm our dignity as human beings. Living out these values in our personal and professional lives is not only good for us as individuals; it is also good for the world around us. When we demonstrate these qualities in our lives, we treat others the way we would each like to be treated. And by doing so, we help others and we make the world a better place.

prepare and give injections and enemas, apply dressings, give alcohol rubs and massages, apply ice packs and hot water bottles, and monitor *catheters*.

LPNs observe patients and report adverse reactions to medications or treatments. They collect samples of blood or other body fluids for testing, perform routine laboratory tests, feed patients, and record food and fluid intake and output. They help patients with bathing, dressing, and personal hygiene, keep them comfortable, and care for their emotional needs. In states where the law allows, they may administer prescribed medicines or start intravenous fluids. Some LPNs help deliver, care for, and feed infants. Experienced LPNs may supervise nursing assistants and aides.

> Guidelines for ethical professional conduct for nurses have been established by:
> - the American Nurses Association,
> - the International Nurses Council,
> - the American Hospital Association,
> - the Canadian Nurses Association,
> - and other nursing organizations.

LPNs in nursing homes provide routine bedside care, help evaluate residents' needs, develop care plans, and supervise the care provided by nursing aides. In doctors' offices and clinics, they also may make appointments, keep records, and perform other clerical duties. LPNs who work in private homes may also prepare meals and teach family members simple nursing tasks.

If you choose a career as a licensed practical nurse, your training lasts about a year and is available in about 1,100 state-approved programs, mostly in vocational or technical schools. All states require LPNs to pass a licensing examination after completing a state-approved practical nursing program. A high school diploma or equivalent usually is required for entry, although some programs accept candidates without a diploma or are designed as part of a high school curriculum.

Most practical nursing programs include both classroom study and supervised clinical practice (patient care). Classroom study covers basic nursing concepts and patient-care related subjects, including

The Canadian Nurses Association has drafted this definition of nursing values:

Safe, competent, and ethical care
Nurses value the ability to engage in nursing care that allows them to fulfill their moral obligations to the people they serve.

Health and well-being
Nurses value health promotion and well-being and assist persons to achieve their optimum level of health in situations of normal health, illness, injury, disability or at the end of life.

Choice
Nurses respect and promote the autonomy of persons and help them to express their health needs and values, as well as to obtain appropriate information and services.

Dignity
Nurses respect the inherent worth of each person they serve and advocate for respectful treatment of all people.

Confidentiality
Nurses safeguard personal and health information learned in the context of a professional relationship, and ensure it is shared outside the health care team only with the person's permission or as legally required.

anatomy, *physiology*, medical-surgical nursing, pediatrics, obstetrics, psychiatric nursing, administration of drugs, nutrition, and first aid. Clinical practice usually is in a hospital, but sometimes includes other settings.

One way to know if a nursing career is right for you is to get involved while you are still in high school. Start by talking with your career or guidance counselor to see what classes you should be taking

Justice
Nurses uphold principles of equity and fairness to assist persons in receiving a share of health services and resources proportionate to their needs and in the promotion of social justice.

Accountability
Nurses are accountable for their practice, and they act in a manner consistent with their professional responsibilities and standards of practice.

Quality Practice Environments
Nurses value and advocate for practice environments that have the organizational and human resources necessary to ensure safety and support for all persons in the work setting.

over the next few years. Classes such as biology, chemistry, psychology, sociology, and math will help prepare you for the advanced training you will need to take in college or nursing school.

Start talking with nurses about their work and qualifications, what a typical day is like, what they like and don't like about their job, and you will be gaining knowledge about the nursing profession. If you are old enough, try to get a part-time job in a hospital. Many hospitals hire high school students for part-time or weekend work. You may be able to get a job as an orderly, helping to transport patients around the hospital, or as a nurse's aide. Even if jobs are not available, check with the hospital to see if they need any volunteers. The more you become familiar with hospitals and nursing, the better informed you will be when it comes to making a career decision.

As you learn about this career, you will be able to assess more realistically if you have what it takes to be a good nurse. In addition to the training you will need, you will need to be the right kind of person for the job. A nurse needs a certain type of personality—and the right sort of character.

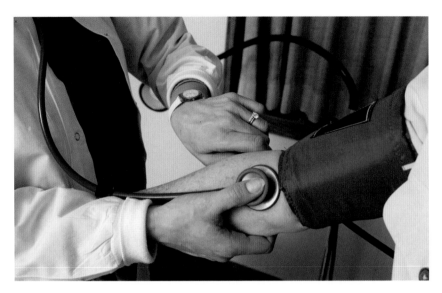

A nurse needs to be able to accurately observe and record patient symptoms and readings.

Your personality may or may not be suited for a career in nursing, and that's something you will need to think about if you are considering this career. For instance, do you possess the physical strength needed for the job? Do you work well under pressure? Are you good with your hands? Nurses also should have keen observational, decision-making, and communication skills. As part of a healthcare team, they must be able to follow orders and work under close supervision. They should be emotionally stable, because work with the sick and injured can be stressful.

But *character* means something a bit different from *personality.* Your personality is often shaped by your environment; it is also influenced by the genetic material you inherited from your biological parents. Character, however, is built on the choices you make. Only *you* can choose how you will make use of your unique package of talents and abilities. No matter what type of nurse you think you want to be— or even if you decide to pursue a totally different career—character is as important to your future profession as the skills you will use to succeed in your job.

If you decide to pursue a career in nursing, expect plenty of occasions when you'll be faced with the chance to choose your character. Because of the nature of their work, all nurses need to possess integrity and trustworthiness, respect and compassion, justice and fairness, responsibility, courage, self-discipline and diligence, and citizenship. These qualities form the foundation for a good character. And in nursing, as in the rest of life, character makes the difference between failure—and true success.

We should strive for what we can best do and what is most attractive and thereby find our duty.

—Florence Nightingale

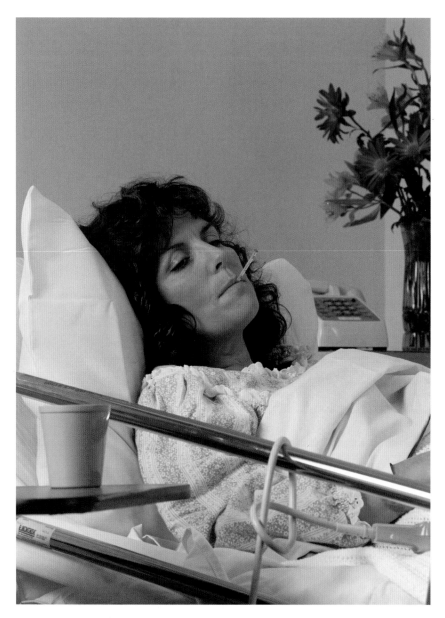

Because nurses deal with people who are at their most helpless, integrity is a necessity.

2

INTEGRITY AND TRUSTWORTHINESS

Knowing right from wrong is not always easy.

Trustworthiness is at the very core of all relationships—and yet it is something we often take for granted in our relationships, both socially and professionally. Healthcare professionals, however, build their practice on the basis of integrity and trust. Lives rest in their hands. Patients need to trust health care providers to be persons of honesty and integrity, persons of high moral and ethical standing.

Nurse Doris Scott was more than weary. The evening had been filled with three admissions, two patients going to surgery, rounds with doctors, and patient call bells that never stopped ringing. Now it was time to get the evening medications to the patients. She wondered if this shift would ever end.

With her thoughts going in many directions, she hurried down the corridor to the patient rooms, giving each person under her care the medications the doctor had ordered. She smiled as she entered Mrs. Shaw's room; the elderly woman was a friend and neighbor who had watched Doris grow up. Seeing an old friend was a pleasant distraction on such a hectic evening. As they chatted, Doris gave the medicine and

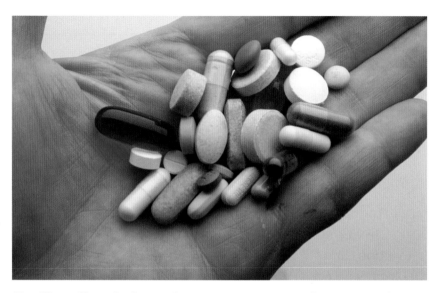

Handling pills and other medications requires care; the wrong medicine for the wrong patient could be dangerous or even life threatening.

When people have integrity:

- They don't tell lies.
- They don't take what isn't theirs.
- They don't cheat.
- They don't hide the truth so they will look better.
- They admit their mistakes and face the consequences.

When people have integrity, others can trust them.

a cup of water to Mrs. Shaw. Once the medicine was taken, Doris left the room and moved on to her next patient.

Suddenly, in the midst of her weariness and confusion, Doris realized she had given the wrong drug to the wrong patient. By mistake, she had administered the next patient's medication to Mrs. Shaw.

Gathering her thoughts, Doris tried to think what she should do next. She checked the drug she had given to her old friend, and with a sigh of relief she realized that one dose of it should not cause any harm. It was a minor error.

The philosopher Immanuel Kant wrote that people have an absolute duty to do the right thing under all circumstances, regardless of the consequences. He saw moral obligations as absolute and invariable, allowing no exceptions or extenuating circumstances. From this perspective, "speaking the truth" and "doing the right thing" are indispensable traits for all people, including nurses.

Other philosophers disagree with Kant. They view truthfulness as preferable to deception, but they view truth not as something absolute; instead, they perceive all truth as being relative. Therefore, they believe there are times when the truth may need to be modified a bit. For them justifiable deception, under certain circumstances, is morally appropriate.

What do you think?

Working the hospital floor during a long night shift is exhausting—but being trustworthy demands that nurses act with integrity even when they are tired.

An ethical dilemma is when we must make a choice between what is right and what is wrong. Sometimes the right course of action is clear—but other times, the situation may be so complicated that no option seems to be obviously the right thing to do. When that's the case, here are some steps to take:

1. Imagine that positions were reversed. How would you want the other person to behave, if they were in your place and you were in theirs?
2. Imagine that your mother or a child to whom you are close will know whatever you decide to do. How would you feel about their reactions to each option?
3. Imagine that your actions will be headline news. Would you be comfortable with the whole world reading about your choice?
4. Go to a friend or older person whose wisdom you trust and ask for help as you sort through your options.

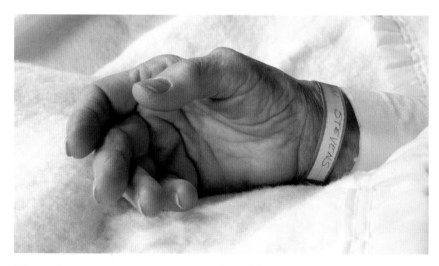

If you choose a career in nursing, vulnerable patients will depend on you to care for them with integrity.

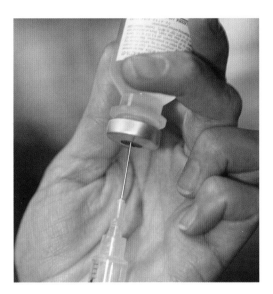

Measuring medications accurately is a vital element of a nurse's trustworthiness.

For the rest of her shift, however, Doris monitored Mrs. Shaw carefully. The older woman showed no ill effects, and Doris decided she had made an error of no consequence. Mrs. Shaw had no signs of any drug reaction during the remainder of the evening.

But Doris knew the hospital ***protocols*** about reporting such incidents:

1. Document the incident in the patient's chart.
2. Report the incident to the charge nurse.
3. Notify the patient's physician, and complete and send an incident report.

Doris told herself, however, that given the hectic workday, her mistake was understandable. If she in-

According to the International Council of Nurses' Code of Ethics, nurses have four fundamental responsibilities in providing nursing care:

1. to promote health.
2. to prevent illness.
3. to restore health.
4. to alleviate suffering.

formed the doctor of the error, he might see her as incompetent. Why should she write out an incident report, when the nature of her mistake did not warrant risking possible serious professional consequences for herself? After all, Mrs. Shaw was fine.

Doris was facing an ethical dilemma. She was unsure of just what to do. Her whole life she had prided herself on her integrity; she certainly knew right from wrong. Yet she hesitated now, almost paralyzed. Where could she go for help to clarify her thinking?

What would you do in her place?

The truth shall set you free.

—Jesus Christ

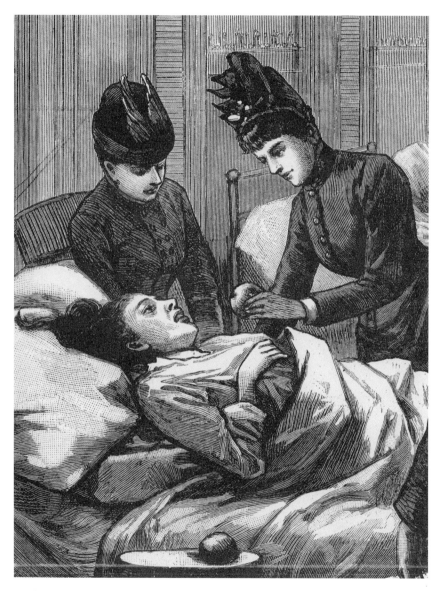

In the 19th century, some wealthy women took up nursing as a form of charity—but nursing was still not considered to be a proper career for women.

3

RESPECT AND COMPASSION

Respect and compassion are powerful
motivations for doing good.

From the time she was a child, Clara Barton cared about others. But she did more than just *feel* compassion—she did something concrete to make life better for those in pain. When she was still a young girl, she was already considered to be very practical. While other girls her age were busy playing with dolls and toys, Clara was busy learning how to sew a dress or how to hammer a nail into a board. For as long as she could remember, she was the type of person who always found a way to meet a need. Her resourcefulness came in handy during the Civil War when she saw wounded Union soldiers in need of food, medical supplies, and blankets. She was quick to organize as many volunteers as she could to donate supplies and services to aid the troops.

Her life of compassionate action began early. When her brother David was helping a neighbor tear down a barn, a wall collapsed on top of David, causing him numerous injuries. Even though Clara was only eleven years old, she was given the job of caring for him. David took nearly two years to recover fully, and during that time Clara did her best to care for him. Other people commented on how responsible Clara was, and they praised her for the respect and compassion she showed to everyone with whom she came in contact. They knew that Clara was

27

When you have respect and compassion for others. . .

- you practice the Golden Rule. In other words, you treat other people the way you would like to be treated.
- you don't take advantage of situations in ways that might benefit you but hurt others.
- you demonstrate your concern for others.

always looking for a challenge to tackle, and by age 15, she began her professional life as a teacher.

Over the next few years Clara Barton continued teaching and even established a few schools all by herself. By 1854, however, she grew weary of teaching and with the help of a family friend, she was able to get a job with the U.S. Patent Office in Washington, D.C. Although she thought she would enjoy that type of work, she still felt that something was missing in her life. She wanted to do something more to help people.

In 1861, when war broke out between the states, Clara Barton suddenly found herself working as a nurse, helping the many wounded sol-

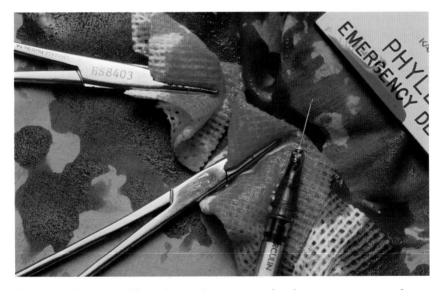

Nurses today (as in Clara Barton's time) need to have strong stomachs for dealing with blood.

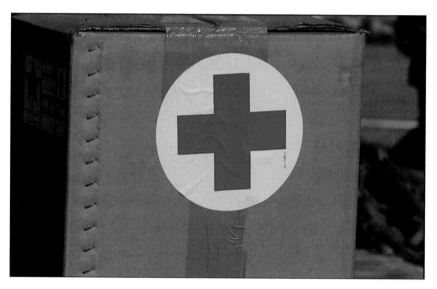

Today the Red Cross continues the work Clara Barton began by sending supplies to war-torn regions.

diers. She was horrified to discover that there weren't enough bandages to treat all of the wounded men, so she began tearing up her own sheets to use as bandages. She even put a notice in the newspaper asking for donations of food, medicine, and bandages. Soon people responded with enough donations, and Clara set up a system of distributing them to the soldiers in need.

One of her systems involved going out directly on the battlefield to deliver medicines and bandages to the wounded soldiers. She ignored the army officers and surgeons who told her to stay away;

Clara Barton was born on Christmas Day in the year 1821 in the town of North Oxford, Massachusetts. Although her parents had named her Clarissa, she preferred to be called Clara. She had four brothers and sisters, but her siblings were all at least ten years older than she was, so she usually had no one with whom to play. Clara spent many hours playing with her pets, pretending they were sick or injured so that she could nurse them back to health.

Clara Barton had many opportunities to make ethical decisions throughout her nursing career. Some of those decisions must have been hard to make, while other times they were easier. She may have used thoughts based on something similar to these four steps to help her reach many of those decisions:

1. *Recognize that there is a moral issue at hand.* This is sometimes the hardest step for people to take. It may seem easier to ignore a problem and hope that it goes away by itself. But problems cannot be ignored; they must be addressed. In Clara Barton's case, she knew she had a moral obligation to treat the wounded soldiers on the battlefield.
2. *Evaluate the situation.* When Clara found out about the wounded soldiers not having enough medicine and bandages, she weighed all of her options and selected the best one.
3. *Make a decision.* In virtually all of her actions, Clara Barton never seemed to hesitate when it came time to make a decision. For instance, her decision to put a notice in the newspaper resulted in many donations of medicines and bandages, which helped thousands of wounded soldiers recover.
4. *Implement and modify.* Once Clara made a decision, she continued to assess the situation. She did not hesitate to call on other people to lend assistance, and she was able to adjust her actions as progress was made.

she saw a need and knew she had to help. Her quest for compassion was a driving force behind her efforts to help the wounded soldiers. During many battles, including Antietam, the second battle of Bull Run, and Fredericksburg, Clara drove a wagon with a team of mules right into the middle of the fighting. According to one story, Clara once held a

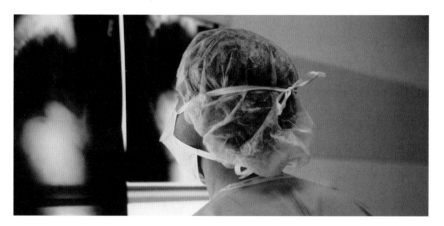

Nurses today have technology (like X rays) that was never imagined in Clara Barton's day.

The Battle of Antietam was fought on September 17, 1862. As the single bloodiest day in the Civil War, more than 23,000 men were killed, wounded, or missing in action. Following this battle, President Abraham Lincoln issued the Emancipation Proclamation.

Antietam National Battlefield was established in 1890. A monument was raised for the "Angel of the Battlefield," which states the following:

CLARA BARTON.
During the battle of Antietam
September 17, 1862
Clara Barton brought supplies
and nursing aid to the wounded
on this battlefield.
This act of love and mercy
led to the birth of the present
AMERICAN
NATIONAL RED CROSS.

In the 19th century, Clara Barton's respect and compassion for the wounded inspired many other women to become nurses.

wounded soldier in one arm and offered him a drink with her other hand. A bullet flew under her arm and killed the soldier. It tore her dress, which she never mended. She kept it as a reminder of why she did her job as a battlefield nurse. If the soldiers could endure mortal danger, so could she.

After a lecture tour and a visit to Europe, Clara Barton returned to the United States and convinced the President to *ratify* the Geneva Convention and form a Red Cross organization. It took her until 1881 to officially establish the American National Red Cross, and she remained its president until 1904. Throughout her life, her concern for others drove her to find practical solutions that would make their life

On April 12, 1912, at the age of 91, Clara Barton passed away at her 38-room home in Glen Echo, Maryland, which for a number of years had served as headquarters for the American Red Cross.

From the American Nursing Association's Code of Ethics for Nurses:

- The nurse's primary commitment is to the patient, whether an individual, family, group, or community.
- The nurse promotes, advocates for, and strives to protect the health, safety, and rights of the patient.

Many people enjoy reenacting Civil War battles. The real-life battles, where Clara Barton nursed the wounded, were some of the bloodiest in American history.

easier. Her passion to serve the sick and injured has inspired many men and women to choose nursing as a career.

Thankfully, most nurses today are not usually called to go on the field of battle, unless they are serving in the armed forces as a health or medical professional. But whether they work in a busy city hospital emergency room—or amid the quieter pace of a nursing home—today's nurses all have something in common with Clara Barton: they have compassion and respect for others . . . and they care enough to do something practical to help. They work hard to ease the pain of those who are sick or suffering.

*By being concerned about your neighbor you make progress on
your journey.*

—Augustine of Hippo

A hospital visit may be painful and traumatic; or, when a new life enters the world, a hospital stay may be joyous and wonderful. Either way, patients are dependent on nurses for care.

4

JUSTICE AND FAIRNESS

Justice and fairness are foundation stones
for good health care.

The ethical principle of justice means giving each person or group of persons what they are due. Fairness and equity are often the standards employed to determine a just decision. In nursing, fairness and equity often focus on a person's access to care and on the allocation of scarce resources for treatment.

Each time a nurse is assigned to care for a patient, a ***covenant*** relationship is established; it is related to the patient's need for care and the nurse's willingness to provide the care. Each side of the relationship has a role to play in the process of determining the diagnosis and choices of treatment. The healthcare team, including the patient, must communicate clearly with one another in sharing information about the patient's health history, current problem, and available treatment options. Only as they fulfill their mutual responsibilities to one another, can fair, just—and effective—care be provided. Patients can receive care that is fair and equitable only if there is open and honest communication, sensitivity to cultural and ethnic diversity, and unquestioning involvement of the patient in the decision-making process for care.

Nurse Long is assigned to care for Mrs. Cross, an older woman complaining of weakness, irregular heartbeats, thirst, and imbalance. Dur-

Alcohol can play a role in many health conditions.

ing the course of the morning care, Nurse Long and her patient talk about Mrs. Cross's concerns. In the course of the conversation, Mrs. Cross reveals that she enjoys a cocktail or two in the evening. She then inadvertently discloses that she has a drink now and then during the day, as well. She says she doesn't keep count of the number of drinks but adds, "It isn't many." The patient asks Nurse Long not to tell anyone else about her "cocktails." The nurse, however, suspects that some of Mrs. Cross's problems could be caused by poor nutrition and excessive use of alcohol.

What should Nurse Long do with what she has learned? Should she respect Mrs. Cross's privacy and keep her secret—or inform Mrs. Cross's doctor so that he can better address her health needs?

Consider the Patient's Bill of Rights as you answer this question:

Right No. 1 states:
The patient has the right to considerate and respectful care.

Right No. 5 states:
The patient has the right to every consideration of privacy. Case discussion, consultation, examination, and treatment should be conducted so as to protect each patient's privacy.

How does justice relate to this situation? What is a fair and equitable response for everyone involved?

Mr. Von Rulka is a concert violinist who was admitted to the hospital through the emergency room after he seriously injured his left hand. He is in need of surgery to repair the injury, and the emergency room physician told him he has two op-

People who value justice and fairness:

- treat all people the same (as much as possible).
- are open-minded; they are willing to listen to others' points of views and try to understand.
- consider carefully before making decisions that affect others.
- don't take advantage of others' mistakes.
- cooperate with others.
- recognize the uniqueness and value of each individual.

Adapted from material from the Character Counts Coalition, 4640 Admiralty Way, Suite 1001, Marina del Rey, California 90292.

As nurses, if we are people of character, we will treat each patient with justice and fairness.

tions for the surgery. One surgical procedure will restore his hand movement so he will be able to play again. This surgery, however, will leave him with considerable wrist pain. The second operation does not have the same success rate for restoration of the hand movement, but it would probably leave him pain free. The doctor has strongly recommended that Mr. Von Rulka have the operation that would leave him free of pain.

Mr. Von Rulka faces a terrible choice. If he agrees to the first operation, will he be able to tolerate the pain and still perform? If he agrees to the second operation and it fails to restore his hand movement, his career could end. Frightened and anxious, he is considering

Some Definitions

According to Merriam-Webster's dictionary, fairness is marked by impartiality and honesty, free from self-interest, prejudice, or favoritism. Justice is the quality of being impartial; it is the ideal of right action.

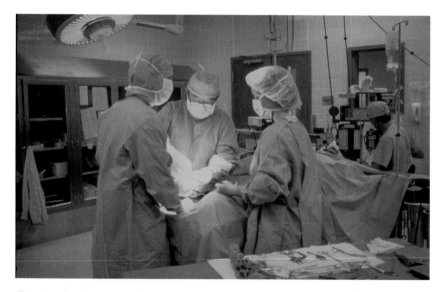

During the trauma of surgery and emergency treatment, patients need nurses to act as their advocates.

Nursing requires an understanding of electronic readings and what they indicate about a patient's condition; but a good nurse also needs justice and fairness, qualities that extend deeper than mere knowledge.

The Patient's Bill of Rights is a covenant document that offers guidance to the patient, the healthcare providers, and health care institution. The bill was designed by the American Hospital Association to express the collaboration necessary to ensure equitable patient care in the hospital setting. This Bill of Rights declares that fairness in the delivery of care needs to be a shared effort between the patient and healthcare providers. Utilization of the 12 rights in the Patient's Bill of Rights is the framework for the provision of fair and equitable services.

asking for a second opinion and even thinking of requesting a transfer to another hospital for treatment. He turns to the nurse who is caring for him and asks what she thinks he ought to do.

His nurse now faces an ethical dilemma. What responses should she make in order to be fair and just? Consider the Patient Bill of Rights as you answer this question:

Right No. 2 states:
The patient has the right to and is encouraged to obtain from physicians and other direct caregivers relevant, current, and understandable information concerning diagnosis, treatment, and prognosis.

Right No. 8 states:
The patient has the right to expect that, within its capacity and policies, a hospital will make reasonable response to the request of a patient for appropriate and medically indicated care and services. When medically appropriate and legally permissible, or when a patient has so requested, a patient may be transferred to another facility. The institution to which the patient is to be transferred must first have accepted the patient for transfer. The patient must also have the benefit of complete information and explanation concerning the need for, risks, benefits, and alternatives to such a transfer.

From the American Nursing Association's Code of Ethics:

The nurse, in all professional relationships, practices with compassion and respect for the inherent dignity, worth and uniqueness of every individual, unrestricted by considerations of social or economic status, personal attributes, or the nature of health problems.

How does justice relate to this issue? What would you do if you were the nurse? If you were the patient, what would you want your nurse to do?

In giving rights to others that belong to them, we give rights to ourselves and our community.

—John F. Kennedy

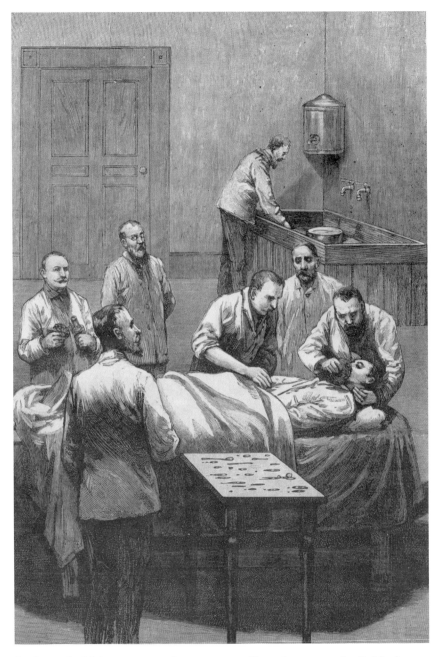

In the early 19th century, only men were allowed to enter the field of medicine. Nursing was not considered an appropriate occupation for well-bred women.

5

RESPONSIBILITY

A sense of responsibility can push people to change the world for the better.

Florence Nightingale could have taken life easy. She and her sister grew up on their parents' country estate where they received the finest education that was available at the time. Their parents wanted them to have the best of everything, and they spared no expense for their daughters. In the 1800s, wealthy young ladies had few responsibilities; they were expected to simply enjoy themselves. Florence, however, never really cared for the life of a rich girl.

Instead, she wished she could care for the sick and help relieve their suffering. She felt she had a responsibility to others—and that strong sense of responsibility inspired her to take action. As often as she could she would visit the sick tenants on her family's estate. She brought them food and helped them to change their bedding, much to the dismay and disapproval of her parents.

Florence told her parents she wanted to visit local hospitals and learn about nursing. Her parents were not happy with her ambition and tried to persuade her from pursuing her dreams. Hospitals in Victorian England were thought of as places where only poor people went to be treated. Wealthy people could afford to have a doctor visit their estate and never worried about hospitals. Her parents tried in vain to get her to travel and attend parties, but nothing was going to stop Florence

Nightingale. She had made up her mind that she was going to learn all about nursing.

Florence was encouraged to care for the sick and the poor by Dr. Samuel Gridley Howe and his wife, Julie Ward Howe, the famous American abolitionists. Florence's mother was active in the antislavery movement and had invited the Howes to visit. Dr. Howe assured Florence that caring for others was indeed a noble thing to do. She was encouraged by his remarks and started visiting local hospitals. But she was shocked when she discovered that many of the English hospitals were filthy and overcrowded.

She also discovered that the nurses had not received any proper training and that the working con-

Being responsible means:

- your behavior shows you can be trusted.
- you deliver what your promise.
- you always do your best.
- you don't make excuses for yourself.

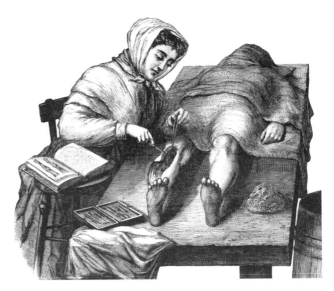

Two hundred years ago, a woman who was interested in anatomy and medicine was considered to be unnatural and shocking. She often had to study secretly.

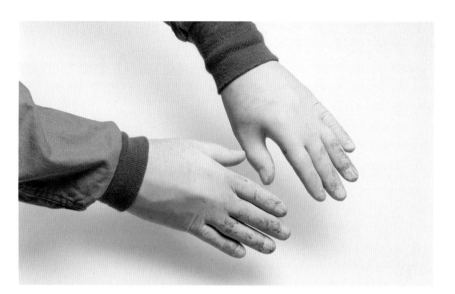

Today we understand that nursing requires sterile conditions. But in Florence Nightingale's day, this was a new and radical concept.

ditions were horrible. Diseases were spreading quickly among the patients and even among the nursing staff as well. After visiting the hospitals a few times, Florence thought about the hospital system and how it needed to be fixed in order to better serve the patients. Even at that young age, she felt a growing sense of responsibility to the nursing profession and to sick and poor people everywhere.

Florence Nightingale was born on May 12, 1820. Her parents were touring Italy at the time and named her for the famous city they were visiting.

During a trip to Europe and Egypt, Florence studied how the sick were being cared for in other countries. One observation that struck her was that patients who were clean and well fed had a much better chance of recovery. She realized that the Roman Catholic nuns in France and the women in the Protestant nursing orders in Germany did a much better job of caring for the sick than nurses did in England. Flo-

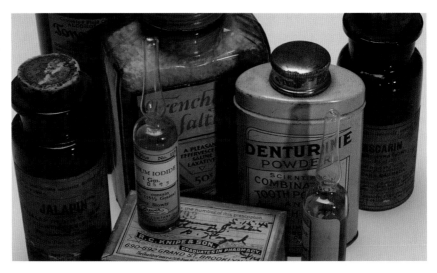

Before the discovery of antibiotics, the medicines available for treating infections were limited and often ineffectual.

Florence Nightingale's Pledge

I solemnly pledge myself before God and presence of this assembly; to pass my life in purity and to practice my profession faithfully.

I will abstain from whatever is deleterious and mischievous and will not take or knowingly administer any harmful drug.

I will do all in my power to maintain and elevate the standard of my profession and will hold in confidence all personal matters committed to my keeping and family affairs coming to my knowledge in the practice of my calling.

With loyalty will I endeavor to aid the physician in his work, and devote myself to the welfare of those committed to my care.

rence was so impressed with a training school for nurses known as the German Institute of Deaconesses that she enrolled there for a four-month nursing course. Later, she studied at hospitals in Paris, and by 1853, she was appointed superintendent of a women's hospital in London. She felt that she was finally meeting her responsibilities by serving the nursing profession and making improvements in the hospital care system.

When war broke out in 1854, the British suffered heavy casualties, and they had no plan in place to care for the wounded soldiers. Newspapers, which were just starting to cover major world events, carried stories about the wounded British soldiers who were left to die terrible deaths in dirty and rat-infested hospitals. The British secretary of war had heard about Florence Nightingale and the work she had done at other hospitals; he asked her if she would try and improve the conditions for treating the wounded soldiers. Florence immediately began to recruit intelligent, able women to help with her new nursing corps.

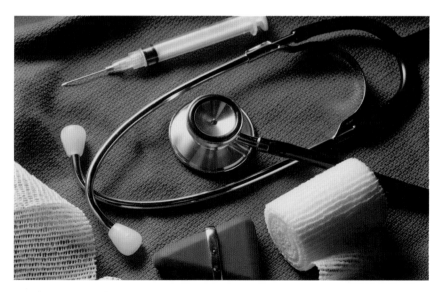

Modern medical instruments and tools were not available to most nurses in Florence Nightingale's time.

From the American Nursing Association's Code of Ethics for Nurses:

- The nurse is responsible and accountable for individual nursing practice and determines the appropriate delegation of tasks consistent with the nurse's obligation to provide optimum patient care.
- The nurse owes the same duties to self as to others, including the responsibility to preserve integrity and safety, to maintain competence, and to continue personal and professional growth.

After signing up nearly 40 women, Florence set off on her journey. She found thousands of wounded soldiers who had been left to care for themselves in horrible conditions. She and the other nurse volunteers cleaned and scrubbed so that the makeshift hospitals would be more sanitary. Florence had a habit of lighting a lantern at night and walking among the wounded soldiers, and soon the legend of the "lady with the lamp" began to grow.

Her responsible efforts to improve conditions for treating the wounded soldiers led to a drop in the death rate from 42 percent in February of 1855 to only 2 percent that June. Florence Nightingale embraced her career with everything she had. After the war she continued to write reports and studies that led to many improvements in the health and sanitation problems in various hospitals around the world. She has been regarded by the entire world as the foremost authority on nursing—and she took responsibility to a new level of caring.

. . . Keep this simple question in [mind]: How can I provide for this right thing to always be done?

—Florence Nightingale

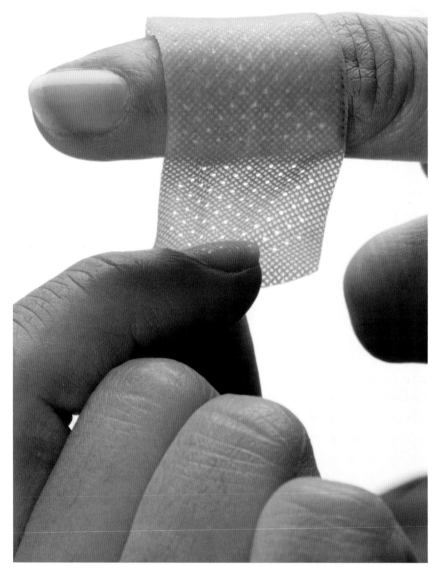

A nurse is anyone who tends a wound or helps a sick person heal.

6

COURAGE

*Courage asks us go where we have never
gone—and gives us the strength to
face the challenge.*

Ever since she was a little girl, Linda Richards had been helping
people who were sick. She did her best to care for her mother, and
after her mother died, Linda continued to care for other people who
were ill and suffering. Linda wanted to become a real nurse, but in the
1800s, no nursing schools would accept her or other women who were
interested in a nursing career.

Doc Currier encouraged Linda, though, to learn as much as she
could. He was the doctor who had helped Linda care for her ailing
mother, and he had noticed how dedicated Linda was and how she was
always there to help in any way she could. After her mother died, Doc
Currier comforted the young girl. He told Linda she had done a fine job
of caring for her mother, but no one, even a skilled nurse, could have
saved her. Linda, however, still wanted to learn more about nursing.
She asked Doc Currier if he would teach her how to treat patients and
help them get well. He told her to come back and see him when she was
a little older.

Doc Currier invited Linda on her 13th birthday to go with him on
some sick calls. Linda was happy that he had remembered her wish,
and in the months to come she worked hard as his helper. Many days

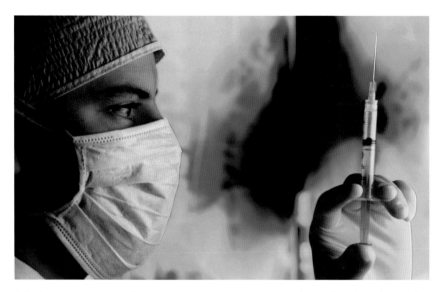

Modern nurses owe their career's existence to Linda Richards, who laid some of the early foundations for nursing in North America.

they would leave at sunrise and not return home until dark. Linda was always asking questions, and she was always eager to learn more about helping sick people feel better and become well.

About six months later, Linda heard a knock at the family farmhouse door. When she and her grandfather answered it, a frantic young man told them his son was very ill and he could not find Doc Currier anywhere. He wanted Linda to come and help him. Linda was scared, but she knew she had to try to help the sick boy.

At the boy's house, she found that little Tommy was too feverish to open his eyes. When Linda saw that Tommy's skin was dry and hot, she tried to remember everything she had from Doc Currier about

People who value courage:

- say what's right (even when no one agrees with them).
- do the right thing (even when it's hard).
- follow their conscience (instead of the crowd).

treating fevers. Swallowing her nervousness, she told the boy's parents they would need plenty of chipped ice and towels. His father hurried outside into the snowy yard to look for chunks of ice. His mother helped Linda prepare the towels for the ice.

A few minutes later, Tommy was covered with towels filled with ice. Throughout the night Linda made sure that when the ice melted it was replaced so that Tommy would be kept cool. She knew from what she had learned from Doc Currier that she had to get the fever lowered. By morning Linda was exhausted, but Tommy appeared to be cooler and more comfortable. With a sigh of relief, Linda realized his fever was finally going away.

When Doc Currier arrived later that day, Linda was glad to see him. She told him she had doubted her abilities to save Tommy—but she had tried not to be afraid when she realized she had a job to do. She couldn't let her fears control her; she had to act to save his life. Doc Currier told Linda she had done everything he would have done—and she had showed great courage under pressure.

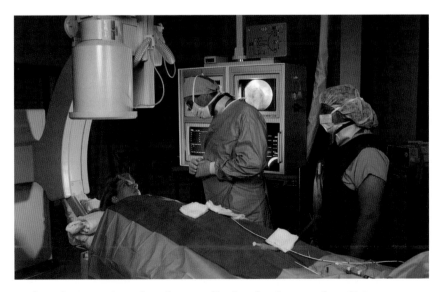

Before the invention of modern medical technology and medicines, even a mild fever could be life threatening.

Three Foundations for Ethical Decision-Making

1. Take into account the interests and well-being of everyone concerned. (Don't do something that will help you if it will hurt another.) In this example, Linda had to decide if agreeing to help the sick boy would be best for everyone involved.
2. When a character value like courage is at stake, always make the decision that will support that value. Just as Linda Richards did, do the right thing even though you may be afraid.
3. Where two character values conflict (for instance, when taking a risk might hurt another person), choose the course of action that will lead to the greatest good for everyone concerned. Be sure to seek all possible alternatives. Don't do something foolhardy simply to prove to the world how brave you are. Courage should be used to support the other core qualities of a good character; in other words, courage needs to be like that Linda Richards demonstrated . . . the kind that is tempered with compassion and respect, integrity, and justice.

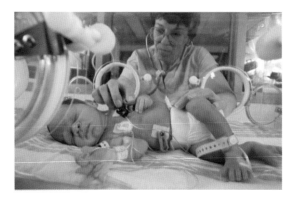

Like Linda Richards, today's nurses courageously fight to save lives—including some of the tiniest and newest lives of all.

Nurses do their jobs with courage. Sometimes this means performing in dramatic, life-saving situations—and other times it means taking a quiet moment to help a patient understand her medical condition.

Linda vowed never to be afraid again when it came time to treat a patient. She refused to let anything stand in her way of helping others, even her own fears. Despite the disapproval and opposition of many, she dedicated herself to becoming a nurse. And in 1873, Linda Richards became America's first woman to graduate from nursing school.

You will have much opposition to encounter. But great works do not prosper without great opposition. . . . Dare to stand alone.

—Florence Nightingale

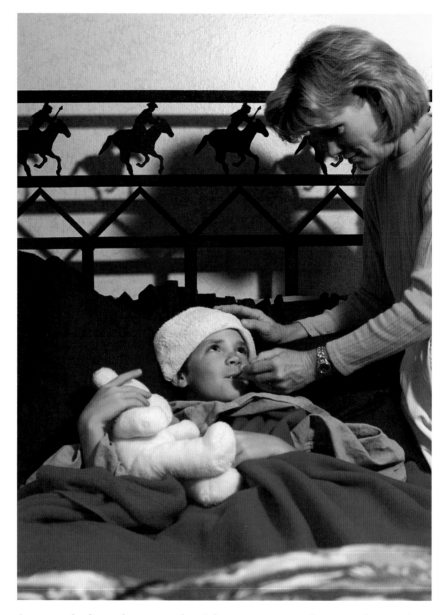

Anyone who has taken care of a sick person, even at home, understands that nursing requires self-discipline and diligence.

7

SELF-DISCIPLINE AND DILIGENCE

*When you possess self-discipline
and diligence, you can accomplish
amazing things.*

Celeste Lewis didn't start her professional career as a nurse. Instead, she first worked as an elementary school teacher, and then left that career to focus on raising her seven children. However, when her youngest child was 12, she had the self-discipline and diligence needed to begin an entire new career. Those same character qualities gave her the push she needed to make it through nursing school—and they are also what make her a diligent and caring nurse today.

Her self-discipline has led her to a life she loves. Celeste has always enjoyed traveling, and today she works as a travel nurse. To be qualified for this position, Celeste needed to exercise her diligence still further, for it requires that she hold nursing licenses in seven states. Her life today is well worth all her hard work, however. "If I can travel the rest of my nursing career, I will," she told NurseZone.com. "Everywhere I go, I have a fresh perspective and know that I am needed."

Being a travel nurse isn't all that Celeste does. She also serves on a travel advisory board and reviews continuing education courses. She is passionate about patient advocacy. "With the recent changes in health care, sometimes the only advocate the patient has is the nurse," Celeste explained. "Making sure the voice of the patient is heard is very impor-

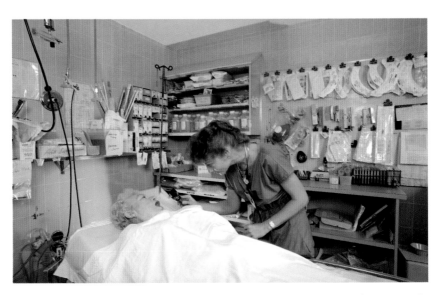

Self-disciplined and diligent nurses have opportunities every day to touch people's lives.

People who value self-discipline and diligence:

- work to control their emotions, words, actions, and impulses.
- give their best in all situations.
- keep going even when the going is rough.
- are determined and patient.
- try again even when they fail the first time.
- look for ways to do their work better.

Adapted from material from the Character Education Network.

tant to me." Her self-discipline and diligence has gained her personal rewards—and it has made a difference to the many sick or injured people she has treated.

Throughout the history of nursing, the hard work, self-discipline, and diligence of many nurses like Celeste Lewis have helped to create today's profession. The American Nurses Association's first president, Isabel Adams Hampton Robb, was the nursing profession's prime mover in organizing at the national level. In 1896, Robb organized the group known as the Nurses' Associated Alumnae of the United States and Canada; the group was renamed the American Nurses Association in 1911, an organization that still exists today. Earlier, in 1893, Robb gathered together a nucleus of women who were superintendents of schools and founded the American Society of Superintendents of Training Schools for Nurses. This organization became the National League of Nursing Education in 1912. Robb was one of the original members of the committee to found the *American Journal of Nursing*. While serving as superintendent of nurses at the Illinois Training School at Chicago and principal of the Training School for Nurses at

Travel nurses are assigned by an agency to a hospital for a working term of eight to 13 weeks. When each term is completed, nurses move on to a new location. Housing is usually provided through the agency. Travel nurse programs were begun in the 1980s to help hospitals deal with their staffing problems.

Some nurses may work in management positions, supervising other nurses. This position will also require self-discipline and diligence.

Johns Hopkins Hospital, Robb initiated many improvements in nursing education. Her self-disciplined diligence was the tool she used to build the nursing profession.

From the American Nursing Association's Code of Ethics for Nurses:

The nurse participates in establishing, maintaining, and improving healthcare environments and conditions of employment conducive to the provision of quality health care and consistent with the values of the profession through individual and collective action.

Champion of the urban poor, Lillian D. Wald was another diligent leader in the nursing field. In 1893, two years after graduation from the New York Hospital Training School for Nurses, Wald founded the forerunner of the Henry Street Settlement. Henry Street eventually evolved into the Visiting Nurse Service of New York City. For more than 40 years, Wald directed the Henry Street Visiting Nurse Service, at the same time constantly opposing political

A diligent nurse takes time to observe patients' symptoms carefully, so that nothing is missed.

Diligence often consists of small things—like being careful to wash your hands thoroughly so as not to spread germs to patients.

and social corruption. She helped initiate revision of child labor laws, improved housing conditions in *tenement* districts, and fought for the enactment of pure food laws, education for the mentally handicapped, and passage of better immigration regulations. Wald was an important part of establishing the United States Children's Bureau, school nursing, and rural nursing in the Red Cross Town and Country Nursing Service. As first president of the National Organization for Public Health Nursing, Wald delivered an inaugural address that suggested a national health insurance plan. She too possessed the diligence and self-discipline necessary to build a more effective nursing profession.

America's first trained nurse, Linda Anne Judson Richards, whose story was told in chapter 6, has long been recognized for her significant innovations in the nursing profession. Richards, who graduated from the New England Hospital for Women and Children in 1873, introduced the concept of keeping patient records, such as nurses' notes and doctors' orders. She also instituted the practice of nurses wearing uniforms. Richards added another "first" to her professional record when she became the first stockholder in the *American Journal of Nursing*. She bought the initial share of stock for $100. Richards served as the first Superintendent of Nurses at Massachusetts General Hospital. In that capacity, she developed the program and proved that trained nurses gave better care than those without formal nurse's training. She brought credit to nursing for her pioneer work in industrial and psychiatric nursing. Throughout her long nursing career, she never stopped working to improve her profession.

Nurses today can be inspired by stories like these. These examples show that self-discipline and diligence have paid off for many nurses over the course of history. These character traits mean that a person is ready to tackle any challenge that comes along. How about you? Do you have what it takes to succeed in a career in nursing? Do you consider yourself to be a person who possesses self-discipline and diligence?

Discipline means power at command. . . . To know what one is to do and move to do it promptly . . . is to be disciplined.

—John Dewey

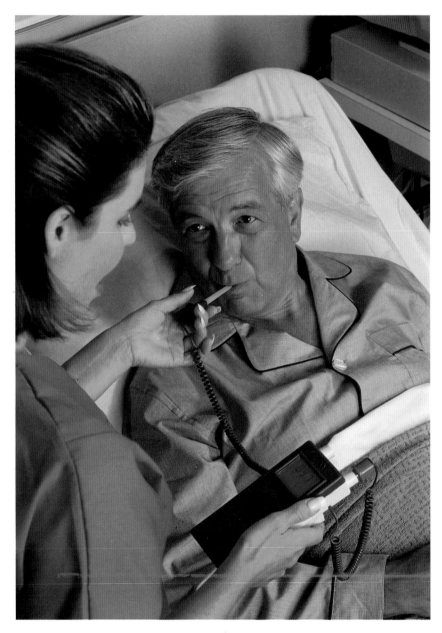

Nurses have many opportunities to volunteer their professional expertise.

8

CITIZENSHIP

Being a good citizen not only means you're law-abiding and pay your taxes—it also means you're involved in some sort of service to your community.

There are literally thousands of examples of nurses and nursing organizations that give back to the community. They are role models of citizenship for others to follow.

Teaming Up to Fight a Serious Disease

Most teenagers don't spend much time worrying about serious illnesses. Teenagers tend to think about the here and now, and forget that today's actions and choices may have serious consequences for the future. That's why volunteer nurses from the University of Michigan Health System (UMHS) and other area health care institutions are taking time to educate kids about hepatitis B. Because of these nurses, students in Michigan have learned that hepatitis B is a serious threat to their lives—and many of them are now immunized against the disease. Through a Michigan Department of Community Health program called "Roll Up Your Sleeves," volunteer nurses from various organizations have teamed up to provide free hepatitis B vaccinations to area middle and high school students. During the 1999–2000 school year, the "Roll

Up Your Sleeves" program immunized 1,204 students at seven schools, and 771 students participated in the program in the 2000–2001 school year. Through this program, middle and high school students at participating schools receive educational seminars and the opportunity to receive the three-shot series of hepatitis B. In the educational seminars, students and their parents learn that hepatitis B is a serious viral disease that attacks the liver and that the virus is spread through blood and other body fluids. Thanks to those volunteer nurses, more students are being educated and saved.

Summer Medical Program

In 1987, actor Paul Newman, with profits from his food company, Newman's Own, donated the major part of the funds needed to build the Hole in the Wall Gang Camp. Nurses who volunteer at this camp have the chance to make a difference in the lives of children.

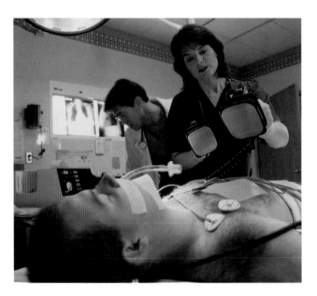

Each time a nurse helps save a life, she is giving a life back to her community.

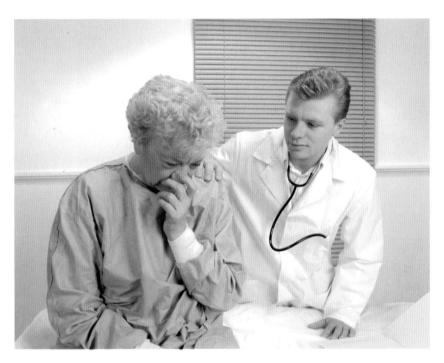

A nurse who takes time to listen to a senior citizen is providing more than just medical care.

Hepatitis B is a virus that is easily passed from one person to another, especially through body fluids; it is 100 times more contagious than the virus that spreads AIDS. Anyone can get hepatitis B, but young adults are at a greater risk. In fact, one out of every 20 people in the U.S. has been infected with hepatitis B. Because of the serious liver disease, cancer, and death resulting from hepatitis B infection, children and teenagers should be vaccinated to protect them before they enter young adulthood when they are most likely to catch hepatitis B. Hepatitis B vaccination is now a required immunization for entrance to kindergarten, and today, vaccination begins with infants at birth.

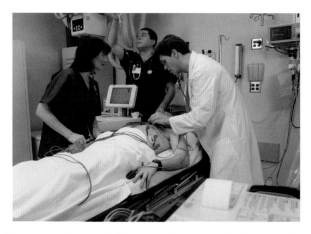

Nurses help protect their neighbors and community in a special way.

According to the Character Counts Coalition, citizenship is:

- playing by the rules.
- obeying the law.
- doing your own share.
- respecting authority.
- keeping informed about current events.
- voting.
- protecting your neighbors and community.
- paying your taxes.
- giving to others in your community who are in need.
- volunteering to help.
- protecting the environment.
- conserving natural resources for the future.

Hole in the Wall doesn't look like a typical medical facility. Instead, the infirmary looks like a 19th-century mill and is called the "OK Corral." At least three staff nurses, two volunteer nurses, and a volunteer doctor join the medical director in providing round-the-clock medical coverage—but they don't look like doctors and nurses either. Instead of white coats, they wear T-shirts and shorts.

So many nurses want to volunteer their time and services at this camp that the waiting list just keeps on growing. Nurses who volunteer for this organization have a chance to give something to their community—and they also find that they

From the American Nursing Association's Code of Ethics for Nurses:

- The nurse participates in the advancement of the profession through contributions to practice, education, administration, and knowledge development.
- The nurse collaborates with other health professionals and the public in promoting community, national, and international efforts to meet health needs.
- The profession of nursing, as represented by associations and their members, is responsible for articulating nursing values, for maintaining the integrity of the profession and its practice, and for shaping social policy.

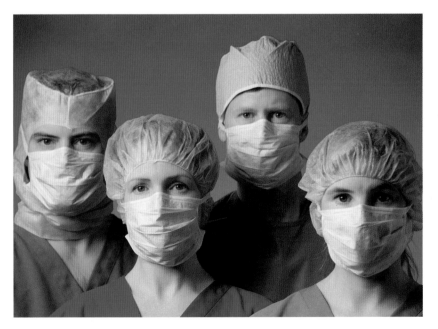

Our communities are safer, better places for us all to live because of the nurses who do their jobs with skill and character.

are personally and professionally renewed and recharged. Citizenship often works that way: when we give something to others, we receive unexpected benefits in return.

Throughout history, nurses have always responded to requests to volunteer their time and expertise. From Florence Nightingale to Clara Barton, from Linda Richards to Isabel Robb, thousands and thousands of nurses have given generously of their time to serve others. These volunteers are true heroes who make a positive difference in a world of sickness and danger. By helping the sick and injured in their communities, they demonstrate their citizenship.

Let us each and all realize the importance of our influence on others—stand shoulder to shoulder—and not alone, in good cause.

—Florence Nightingale

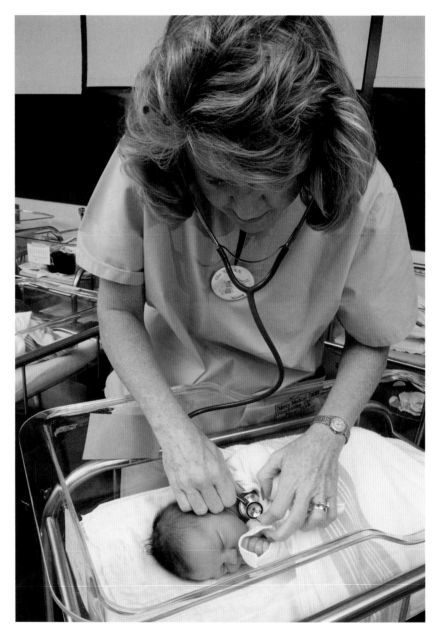

Obstetric nurses care for newborns and their mothers.

9

CAREER OPPORTUNITIES

*Be sure not to miss out on
life's best opportunities.*

John Redthunder loves his job as a nurse in a critical care center. Every day he has the opportunity to help people who are facing health crises. Each shift is different: one day he may spend soothing a frightened child who was in a car accident; the following day he may counsel teenagers who contracted a ***venereal disease***; and on yet another day he may rush back and forth between an elderly woman suffering from smoke inhalation and an emergency delivery of twins. The pace of his work is sometimes exhausting—but John is confident he has the strength of character necessary to take advantage of nursing's many opportunities.

Nurses like John face varied employment opportunities, depending on whether they are RNs or LPNs. Both, however, are growing occupational fields.

Employment Outlook for Registered Nurses

Job opportunities for RNs are expected to be very good. Employment of registered nurses is expected to grow faster than the average for all occupations through 2010, and because the occupation is very large, many new jobs will result. This faster than average growth will be

As the number of older people in the population grows, patient numbers will increase as well, since older people tend to have more health problems.

driven partly by technological advances in patient care, which permit a greater number of medical problems to be treated, and an increasing emphasis on preventive care. In addition, the number of older people, who are much more likely than younger people to need nursing care, is projected to grow rapidly.

Employment in hospitals, the largest sector, is expected to grow more slowly than in other healthcare sectors. While the intensity of nursing care is likely to increase, requiring more nurses per patient, the number of inpatients (those who remain in the hospital for more than 24 hours) is not likely to increase much. Patients are being discharged earlier and more procedures are being done on an outpatient basis, both in and outside hospitals. However, rapid growth is expected in hospital outpatient facilities, such as those providing same-day surgery, rehabilitation, and ***chemotherapy***.

Employment in home healthcare is expected to grow rapidly. This trend is caused by the growing number of older persons with disabilities, as well as by people's preference for care in the home, combined with technological advances that make it possible to bring increasingly sophisticated treatments into the home. The type of care demanded will require nurses to perform complex procedures.

Employment in nursing homes is expected to grow faster than average due to increases in the number of elderly, many of whom require long-term care. In addition, the financial pressure on hospitals to discharge patients as soon as possible should produce more nursing home admissions. Growth in units that provide specialized long-term rehabilitation for stroke and head injury patients or that treat Alzheimer's victims also will increase employment.

An increasing proportion of sophisticated procedures, which once were performed only in hospitals, are being performed in physicians' offices and clinics, including ambulatory surgicenters and emergency medical centers. Accordingly, employment is expected to grow faster than average in these places as healthcare in general expands.

In today's medical world, nurses may rotate among employment

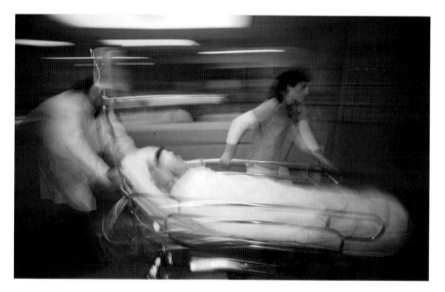

Nurses frequently encounter high-pressure situations.

settings. Because jobs in traditional hospital nursing positions are no longer the only option, RNs will need to be flexible. Opportunities should be excellent, particularly for nurses with advanced education and training.

Employment Outlook for Licensed Practical Nurses

As for RNs, employment of LPNs, especially in nursing homes, is expected to grow through 2010. LPNs seeking positions in hospitals may face competition, as the number of hospital jobs for LPNs declines. However, employment of LPNs is projected to grow much faster than average in places such as clinics, medical centers, and doctors' offices, as healthcare expands outside the traditional hospital setting.

Salaries

Some nurses feel they are not paid enough. Nursing has its hazards, especially in hospitals, nursing homes, and clinics where nurses may care for individuals with infectious diseases. Nurses must observe rigid guidelines to guard against disease and other dangers, such as those posed by radiation, chemicals used for sterilization of instruments, and anesthetics. In addition, they are vulnerable to back injury when moving patients, shocks from electrical equipment, and hazards posed by compressed gases. Many nurses, especially in Canada, are dissatisfied with the relatively low pay they receive in return for facing

These are just some of the special areas of nursing that offer employment opportunities:

- administrative
- community health
- correctional facilities
- emergency/trauma
- forensics
- geriatrics
- government
- intensive care
- mother/baby care
- military
- oncology
- operating room
- parish nursing
- pediatrics
- psychiatric
- research
- school nursing

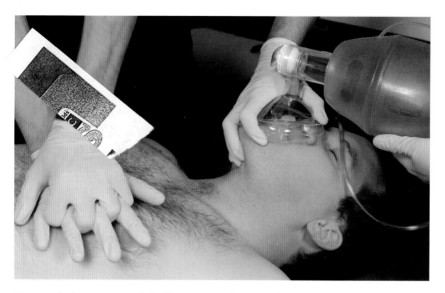

Nurses help save people's lives every day—and yet many nurses are underpaid for this vital work.

these dangers. As a result, some nurses leave their field in favor of other professions. This turnover creates new openings for those entering the field.

Nurses' salaries are growing—but they are still much less than a doctor's salary. Doctors have more years of schooling, of course, but some nurses feel they work as long and hard as any doctor; years of experience also give nurses practical skills a doctor may not possess. The continuing gap between doctors' and nurses' pay scales—and the greater prestige and respect that doctors command—causes some nurses to feel frustrated and bitter.

Money is an important consideration when you are choosing a ca-

Forty years ago, few males considered a career in the nursing field. All of that has changed today, and although only about 6 percent of the nurses in the United States and Canada are male, that number has been slowly increasing over the past decade.

According to the United States Department of Labor's *Occupational Outlook Handbook*, registered nurses make up the largest healthcare occupation, with more than 2 million jobs. Nursing is one of the ten occupations projected to have the largest numbers of new jobs, and job opportunities are expected to be very good. Nursing homes will offer the most new jobs, as applicants in hospitals may face competition as the number of hospital jobs for LPNs declines. Earnings are above average, particularly for nurses who have additional education or training.

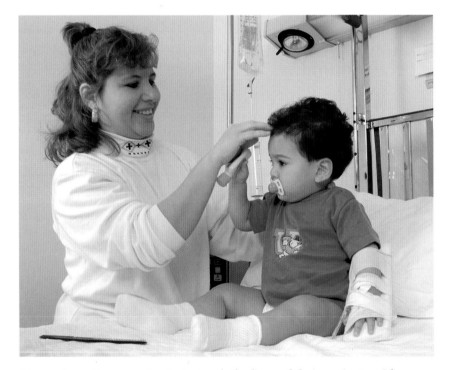

Nurses have the opportunity to touch the lives of their patients with integrity, respect, justice, responsibility, courage, diligence, and good citizenship. They make a difference!

reer. But remember—money isn't everything. As you think about whether nursing is right for you, consider the following scenarios:

> Nursing payscales in Canada have led to labor disputes all across the country. Many Canadian nurses are leaving for other countries, or leaving the profession altogether. It's estimated that there are more than 20,000 Canadian nurses working in the United States. In the state of Hawaii, one out of every eight nurses is Canadian. At least 10 percent of new nursing graduates in Canada head to the United States every year.

- Wilhelmina Brown was dying. She knew she had only a few more weeks to live—but she wasn't scared. Instead, she intended to treasure each of the days she had left. Some days, though, her determination wavered, and she would start to feel frightened or depressed. On those days, she depended on the strength of Sharon Yoon, her home health care nurse. Sharon's cheerful gentleness always brightened Wilhelmina's day. Sharon helped Wilhelmina appreciate the little things in life—like the sun shining through her window, the scent of the daffodils on the stand beside her bed, or the taste of gingerbread for dessert. While Sharon's hands eased the pain in Wilhelmina's body, her smile lifted Wilhelmina's spirit. The nurse made a difference in Wilhelmina's life.

- Ten-year-old Scott Warner wasn't dying like Wilhelmina. But he had been in the hospital a long time, ever since a serious car accident left him in a body cast. While his body healed, Scott was often bored and frustrated; sometimes he was scared and homesick; and other times he felt discouraged and sad, afraid that he would never be back to normal. One of his nurses, Sam Finkelstein, always seemed to understand just how Scott was feeling. Scott looked forward to Sam's shifts. He knew Sam would make his aching body more comfortable—and Sam always had a new joke to make Scott laugh. Sam made a difference in Scott's life.

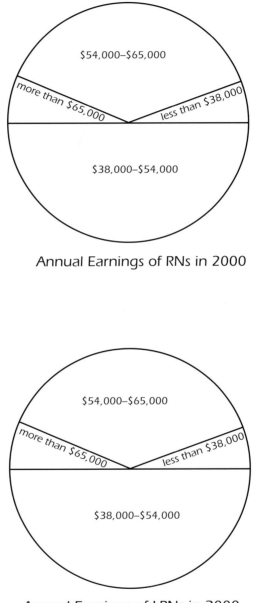

Annual Earnings of RNs in 2000

Annual Earnings of LPNs in 2000

Based on information from the U.S. Department of Labor.

Median annual earnings in the industries employing the largest numbers of *licensed practical nurses* in 2000 were as follows:

- Personnel supply services $35,750
- Home health care services   31,220
- Nursing and personal care facilities   29,980
- Hospitals   28,450
- Offices and clinics of medical doctors   27,520

Median annual earnings in the industries employing the largest numbers of *registered nurses* in 2000 were as follows:

- Personnel supply services $46,860
- Hospitals   45,780
- Home health care services   43,640
- Offices and clinics of medical doctors   43,480
- Nursing and personal care facilities   41,330

If you choose a career in nursing, you too will have countless opportunities to make a difference in the lives of people like Wilhelmina and Scott. Each and every day you will have the chance to demonstrate:

- integrity by dealing honestly with patients so that you earn their trust.
- respect and compassion by aiding those who are sick and suffering.
- justice by ensuring that each patient receives treatment that is fair and equitable.
- responsibility by doing your best to help others who need you.
- courage by daring to face crises with strength and kindness.

How Did I Live Today?

Thomas Shanks, S.J., Ph.D., Executive Director of the Markkula Center for Applied Ethics, recommends that everyone ask themselves these five questions at the end of the day.

- Did I practice any virtues (e.g., integrity, honesty, compassion)?
- Did I do more good than harm?
- Did I treat others with dignity and respect?
- Was I fair and just?
- Was my community better because I was in it? Was I better because I was in my community?

- self-discipline and diligence by always seeking to improve your skills.
- citizenship by making your community a healthier, safer place to live.

Remember, whatever career you choose—character counts!

We are learners and mentors.
We are leaders and scholars.
We are researchers and clinicians.
We are the healing heart and certain hope.
We are nurses.
—Sigma Theta Tau, Honor Society of Nursing

Where your work is, there let your joy be.

—Tertullian

FURTHER READING

Camenson, Blyth. *On the Job: Real People Working in Health Careers.* Lincolnwood, Ill.: VGM Career Horizons, 1996.

Hill, Signe and Helen F. Howlett. *Success in Practical Nursing.* Philadelphia: Saunders Publishing, 1997.

Josephson, Michael S. and Wes Hanson, editors. *The Power of Character.* San Francisco: Jossey-Bass, 1998.

Kelly, Lucie. *Dimensions of Professional Nursing.* New York: McGraw-Hill, 1995.

Kidder, Rushworth M. *How Good People Make Tough Choices.* New York: Simon & Schuster, 1995.

Small, Hugh. *Florence Nightingale, Avenging Angel.* New York: St. Martin's, 1998.

FOR MORE INFORMATION

American Association for the History of Nursing
P.O. Box 175
Lanoka Harbor, NJ 08734
www.aahn.org

American Nurses Association
600 Maryland Avenue, SW
Suite 100 West
Washington, DC 20024-2571
www.ana.org

Canadian Nurses Association
50 Driveway
Ottawa, ON
K2P 1E2 Canada
www.cna-nurses.ca

Character Education Network
www.charactered.net

Discover Nursing
www.discovernursing.com/

Josephson Institute of Ethics
www.josephsoninstitute.org

Nursing World, Online Journal of Issues in Nursing
www.nursingworld.org/ojin/

Publisher's Note:
The Web sites listed on this page were active at the time of publication. The publisher is not responsible for Web sites that have changed their address or discontinued operation since the date of publication. The publisher will review and update the Web sites upon each reprint.

GLOSSARY

Alzheimer's disease A disease of the central nervous system that causes mental degeneration.

Anatomy The study of organisms' (usually humans') physical structure.

Catheters Tubes inserted into blood vessels to allow for the injection of fluids.

Chemotherapy The use of chemicals to treat diseases (often cancer).

Convalescence Recovery period.

Covenant A solemn and binding promise or agreement between two parties.

Obstetric Having to do with birth or pregnancy.

Pediatrics The branch of medicine that treats children.

Physiology A branch of biology that studies the function and activity of living matter (such as cells, tissues, and organs).

Protocols Sets of procedures or rules that govern a particular situation.

Psychiatric Having to do with the branch of medicine that studies mental, emotional, or behavioral disorders.

Ratify To formally approve or confirm.

Regimens Systematic plans (such as a diets, therapies, or medications) designed to improve and maintain patients' health.

Surgicenters Medical centers that specialize in surgical treatments.

Tenement Apartment buildings that are usually run down and crowded.

Venereal disease Contagious illnesses that are spread sexually.

INDEX

BIOGRAPHIES

Rae Simons has written three novels. She also has ghostwritten many books, helping authors find the right words for their stories.

Viola Ruelke Gommer graduated from Columbia University in New York City, College Misericordia in Northeast Pennsylvania, and attended Rutgers University. Her nursing practice has been within schools, hospitals, clinics, nursing homes, and community health agencies in the United States and countries around the world. She is the mother of two and grandmother of six.

Cheryl Gholar is a Community and Economic Development Educator with the University of Illinois Extension. She has a Ph.D. in Educational Leadership and Policy Studies from Loyola University, and she has more than 20 years of experience with the Chicago Public Schools as a teacher, counselor, guidance coordinator, and administrator. Recognized for her expertise in the field of character education, Dr. Gholar assisted in developing the K–12 Character Education Curriculum for the Chicago Public Schools, and she is a five-year participant in the White House Conference on Character Building for a Democratic and Civil Society. The recipient of numerous awards, she is also the author of *Beyond Rhetoric and Rainbows: A Journey to the Place Where Learning Lives.*

Ernestine G. Riggs is an Assistant Professor at Loyola University Chicago and a Senior Program Consultant for the North Central Regional Educational Laboratory. She has a Ph.D. in Educational Leadership and Policy Studies from Loyola University, and she has been involved in the field of education for more than 35 years. An advocate of teaching the whole child, she is a frequent presenter at district and national conferences; she also serves as a consultant for several state boards of education. Dr. Riggs has received many citations, including an award from the United States Department of Defense Overseas Schools for Outstanding Elementary Teacher of America.